Twenty Words

That Will Change Your Life Forever

Establishing
Life Changing
Core Values

By Mark Cress

Founder / President, Corporate Chaplains of America

Twenty Words That Will Change Your Life Forever
By Mark Cress
Copyright ©2005 Mark Cress

ISBN 0-9762151-2-8
For Worldwide Distribution
Printed in the U.S.A.

Lanphier Press
U.S.A.
www.lanphierpress.com

Cover design and layout by Robin Crabtree

Dedicated To:

My Precious Linda

Table of Contents

"INTRODUCTION"

*I*n the early days of building Corporate Chaplains of America for the glory of Jesus in the workplace, we adopted a mission statement for the organization that stands basically unchanged: "To enter the workplace and build relationships with employees with the hope of gaining permission to share the life changing Good News of Jesus Christ in a non-threatening manner." Not long after this, the following corporate vision statement was adopted by our team: "To establish a team of over 1,000 full time chaplains serving over one million employees by 2012." Through the years, we have had a lot of fun incorporating these two themes into the life of our work. At least once a year we would have a contest to see which chaplain could say the mission statement with the most full-size marshmallows in his or her mouth. A record set by Chaplain Jerry Weaver of our Atlanta team in the late 1990s still stands at 31. Trust me – you would have to have seen it to believe it!

Not long after we adopted these statements, it occurred to me that reaching them would require God's anointing and a set of "core values" in my life equal to the task. I prayed and asked God to give me an internal vision for the values He wanted for me and our chaplains. It wasn't long until the 20 words that are the foundation for this book began to stir in my heart. I committed them to paper and glued them onto a piece of cardboard about the size of a business card. Many times a day, I would look at the card and ask God to allow me to actually live them out in my life. At our very next meeting with our chaplain staff, I made a similar card for each chaplain and held a brief training session about the concept of our holding individual "core values".

Much time has passed since that first day when I began to carry the "Mark's Core Values" card. I now have these "Twenty Words That Will Change Your Life Forever" printed on the back of my own business cards. My desire is to have them be clearly integrated into my character. Although there have been times in the past when I have failed them, having these "core values" as a very personal part of my life has never failed me. Looking back, it is the times when I am walking closest to Jesus and am most faithful to these 20 words that represent my happiest and most fulfilling moments as a husband, dad, ministry leader, and friend.

I recommend you begin this journey as I did, prayerfully asking God to use the simplicity of these 20 words to establish Himself more deeply in the routines of your daily life. My greatest prayer for you is that He will honor that prayer and give you peace that passes all understanding and joy unspeakable and full of his Glory.

*F*orget about any misconceptions you may have about books and Bible studies. This book is designed to help you make a genuine change in your life that will last forever. So throw out any old ideas and start with a clean slate.

Step One:
In a conversation with God (a prayer) right now, ask Him to use the words of this book to make a change in your life that will be worth a million times the effort you put into it. The prayer might go something like this:
"Lord Jesus, use the words on these pages and your Word in this book to transform my life. Through your Holy Spirit, take me to a new level of relationship with you, my family, and my friends. Place in me a set of lifetime "core values" that will cause others to want what they see in my life."

Step Two:
Forget seeing this book as some kind of quick read, one night stand, "fix me date". Instead, dedicate one week of your life to becoming immersed in each of the "core values". Focus in on how God can use each value to transform your life forever.

Step Three:
Find a friend or group of friends to go through this process with you. Write in the book ... really "dog ear" it up. Have a goal that by the time you finish the book, it will look like it has been with you on a journey around the world and has the travel scars to show for it.

Step Four:
Commit in your heart right now to stay with the project until God has completed his work of placing a real set of lifetime "core values" in your life. Expect results and use positive "self talk" to stay motivated to see the project though. God cannot wait to work with you in this process. However, you should also expect opposition. Satan is real and is not excited about any of us drawing closer to God or having any values in our life, much less a genuine set of spiritual "core values."

Step Five:
Set a goal for completion. Look at a calendar right now and see what the date will be 11 weeks from now. Write that date in this book and ask God to help you finish this spiritual project by that date.

Now get after it! My prayer is that through the investment of your time and energy with this book, God will manifest Himself in your life in ways you could never imagine. I pray that He will use you as an agent of change in a hurting world that needs Him desperately, and that He will surprise and amaze you to the point that your life will never be the same again.

Blessings,

Mark Cress

April 2005

— Chapter One —

Core Value Number One
"Trust God"

*"Trust in the Lord with all your heart, lean not
on your own understanding, in all your ways
acknowledge Him and He will direct your paths."*
Proverbs 3:5-6

"TRUST GOD"

Sometimes we just don't "get it", do we? We aren't really sure what God is up to in our lives or anywhere else in the world for that matter. A phrase that became heavily used in the early days of the information age probably said it best: There are times when we "just don't know what we don't know". Other times are even more interesting. These are the times when we think we know so much that we become blinded to what is truly in our best interest. Whatever the case, it is often difficult to fully trust God for His perfect will for our lives. In one form or another, many times we revel and even thrive on being control freaks. Who knows when this really starts in our lives? Maybe it's that first time we stand at the end of the diving board at the swimming pool and decide not to jump into the deep water. Or the time as a child when one of our parents is coaxing us to jump into their arms from what seems like the top of Mount Everest, and instead of jumping into the arms of a loving parent, we hesitate and crawl down on our bellies, never to jump again. Who knows or even cares when it starts? The fact is that for most of us, it does, and at that moment we begin a lifelong process of holding back. All the while, God is there saying, "Jump, jump, jump! I'll never let you down. I'll be here no matter what. Jump, for crying out loud!"

It took a while, but the greatest businessman who ever lived, Solomon, finally "got it" when he said: *"Trust in the Lord with all your heart, lean not on your own understanding, in all your ways acknowledge Him and He will direct your paths."* (Proverbs 3:5-6) Think about the context of this statement for a moment. Business leaders pay hundreds of thousands of dollars for consulting advice of all kinds, and right here in just a few words we get the wisest of counsel from one of the greatest business guys of all time and it's totally free. This is the advice from a person who had it all, did it all, saw it all, and practically knew it all. As much as it worked for him thousands of years ago, it will still work for us today and therefore becomes the cornerstone for the "core values" of our lives. The day we finally decide to "give up, let go, and let God" sets the stage for opening the door of God's richest blessings in our lives. It may take a lot of control to give up control, but a lifetime of "joy" (one of the fruits of the Spirit) will certainly be the result. God is real, God is true, and He only wants the very best for you. He is our only safety net in this world. What is keeping us from really trusting Him for every aspect of our lives?

Let's explore a few possibilities together before we decide to totally give up on our controlling ways:

1. Do you think Solomon and the words of the Bible are trustworthy for today? Why or why not?

2. What kind of problems do my control freak tendencies cause with family, friends, work associates, and others?

3. Am I sick and tired of trying to be the glue that holds my entire universe together? What can I do about it?

4. What will it really cost me to totally give control of everything that happens in my life to God?

- _____
- _____
- _____
- _____

5. How would my life be better if I took Solomon's consulting advice from Proverbs?

- _____
- _____
- _____
- _____

——————— Core Verses ———————

📖 Trust God while you are waiting. (Psalm 27:13-14)

📖 Nothing is too hard for God. (Jeremiah 32:17, 26-27)

📖 Simply trust God. (Psalm 37:3, Psalm 42:5)

📖 God cares for people who put their trust in Him. (Nahum 1:7)

Action Steps for Implementing the Core Value
———— "TRUST GOD" ————

𝕴 Start today. Remember the old Chinese proverb, "The journey of a thousand miles begins with one step." Take the first step today. Start telling yourself, your family and your friends that you are "letting go and letting God" have total control of your life.

𝕴 Encourage a friend to join the journey with you.
List three possible friends: • _____

• _____

• _____

𝕴 Make a list of the things in your life you try to control and then talk to God about helping you break your bad habits of being a control freak.

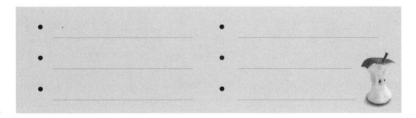

• _____   • _____

• _____   • _____

• _____   • _____

𝕴 Practice the discipline of silence before God. Start with just five minutes once a day. In doing this, you are starting the process of giving up control of the most precious thing you try to control: your time. Listen for God to speak in your heart!

𝕴 Start every day, while still lying in bed, by voicing a prayer asking God to be in total control of every aspect of your life.

PRAYER:

"Lord Jesus, overpower my will to be in control and allow me to totally trust you every minute of this day." Amen.

JOURNAL FOR THE WEEK:

"Trust God for great things; with your five loaves and two fishes, He will show you a way to feed thousands."
– Horace Bushnell

Chapter Two

Core Value Number Two

"Love People"

"Jesus replied: 'Love the Lord your God with all your heart and with all your soul and with all your mind. This is the first and greatest commandment and the second is like it: love your neighbor as yourself.'"
Matthew 22:37-39

"LOVE PEOPLE"

*H*ow can this be so hard? Well, to start with, sometimes God's greatest creation can sometimes be a big pain in the "you know what". People do not always love in return, do they? An example of this is the time the little old granny made a trip to the shopping mall. It was Christmas time and the mall parking lot was packed. She finally spotted a space and just as she was about to pull in, a couple of young boys in a flashy new Corvette slipped in the space ahead of her, jumped out of their shiny car, and yelled at granny, "Hey old girl, that's just what it's like to be young and fast, see ya, wouldn't want to be ya." Just about the time they made it to the entrance of the mall, they turned at the sound of crashing metal only to see granny ramming the Corvette with her Lincoln and then backing up and ramming it again. As they ran to her car screaming, "What are you doing, old woman?" she rolled down her window, handed them a business card and said, "Here is the card for my lawyer, and this is what it's like to be old and slow and rich."

Sure, this is a funny story, but it doesn't really teach us anything about loving people. Quite the contrary is true. But in this chapter's Bible text, Jesus teaches a lesson only a true genius could perform. This, by the way, illustrates the true essence of the genius of Jesus in the first place, which simply put is His uncanny ability to reduce the most complicated subjects on earth to the ridiculously sublime in a matter of seconds. Jesus did it all the time. Remember when He was challenged with the question, "Why are you here?" Most people would have needed as many words as the entire Bible contains to answer this question. Yet, He simply replied, "I'm here so you can have abundant life." Well, as it relates to today's core value, "Love People", He does it once again. How can we truly love people? Jesus makes it as easy as learning how to count to two. He instructs us to first love God, then love people. Many of us have never really learned how to love people because we have not learned how to love God first. Until we learn how to truly love God, we will most likely never learn how to love people. The Bible is very clear: "God is love." This begs a great question: "Is loving God a learned skill or a supernatural process?" Most likely, the answer is both, and the sooner we get about the process, the sooner we will reap the benefits of yet another fruit of the Spirit. Yes, becoming one with Jesus commands us to extend to others. You know, it really is as simple as learning to count to two. All we need to do is (1) "Learn to love God" and (2) "Learn to love people."

Let's explore a few thoughts about loving God and loving people:

1. Have you ever really told God you love Him, short of singing the words in a song at church? Does the concept seem strange to you? List a few love sentences to God here.

2. Have you ever felt God's expression of love toward you? When and how?

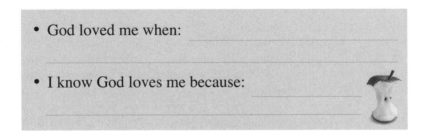

- God loved me when:

- I know God loves me because:

3. Who are some people in life you have truly loved?

4. Is there a person or groups of people you see as totally unlovable?

- _____
- _____
- _____
- _____

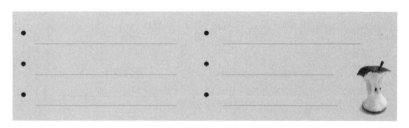

5. What does the thought of God withholding His love from you feel like? List one or two word phrases that best describe your thoughts here (i.e. scary, sad, frightened, etc.):

- _____   • _____
- _____   • _____
- _____   • _____

──────────── Core Verses ────────────

📖 We should love God. (Deuteronomy 6:4-7)

📖 Jesus' command to love God and people. (Matthew 22:37-39)

📖 Love people deeply. (1 Peter 1:22)

📖 Sincere love. (Romans 12:9-10)

📖 The love chapter of the Bible. (1 Corinthians 13)

Action Steps for Implementing the Core Value
—————— "LOVE PEOPLE" ——————

Every day just as you wake up, while still lying in bed, let the first words from your mouth and the first thought in your head be: "I love you, Lord Jesus."

Have a goal to tell at least one person a day that you love them.

Take your Bible and study every scripture in context that contains the word "love". The NIV Bible lists 1,282 references to the word "love".

Make a "Love Prayer List" of all the people you love or who you know love you and commit them to daily prayer. In this prayer, ask God to multiply the list.

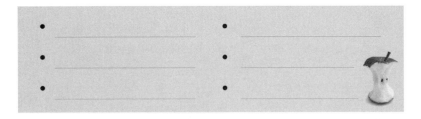

Make a prayer list of people you feel are personally unlovable by you at this time, and ask God to work in your heart and theirs to "shrink" their numbers.

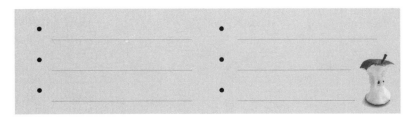

PRAYER:

"Lord Jesus, forgive me for failing to express my love for you in the past and help me to better love people today." Amen.

JOURNAL FOR THE WEEK:

"All loves should be simply stepping stones to the love of God. So it was with me; and blessed be His Name for His great goodness and mercy." – Plato

Chapter Three

Core Value Number Three
"Cherish Family"

"If anyone does not provide for his relatives, and especially for his immediate family, he has denied the faith and is worse than an unbeliever."
I Timothy 5:8 (NIV)

———— "CHERISH FAMILY" ————

You have to let the words of this passage really sink in for a few minutes in order to capture the full essence of their meaning in our lives. Very few commands in the Bible make this kind of dramatic contrast. If we do not cherish our families, we have denied our faith and become worse than unbelievers. Wow! There are other family-related Biblical texts offering more positive promises, like one of the 10 commandments in Exodus 20 that commands us to love our fathers and mothers and that if we do, our days will be long on the earth. Or the passage in Proverbs 22 that tells us to raise our children right so that when they are old, they will still be decent people.

To cherish something is to truly hold it near and dear to your heart. You may have been raised in a nurturing family environment, and therefore the concept of cherishing family doesn't seem all that difficult. On the other hand, you may have suffered quite the reverse and come from a less than loving or even abusive home environment, and the concept of cherishing family is hard to get your arms around. If this is the case, take heart because you really can break the generational pattern and succeed in cherishing family. Our hero and living God, Jesus, made us many promises, a couple of which are worth repeating here. In John 10, He said, "I have come so you can have life and have it more abundantly." And in John 16, He tells us that this world is a crazy, mixed up place that is going to give us trouble, but He concludes with the good news that He has overcome the world on our behalf.

Maybe you are a single parent who stresses with the guilt of feeling like you are forced to neglect your kids to make a living. Or you may be a busy business executive who travels so much you rarely see your family. Marital separation or divorce may be causing you to feel that you can't possibly cherish family ever again. Maybe you are single and the mere conversation about cherishing family hurts. Stop! Stop! Stop! No matter what has happened in the past, through Christ Jesus you can be an overcomer in this vital area of life. With God's help, you can do anything. You have to believe that because it is promised in the Bible and the Bible is never wrong! The Holy Spirit empowered a doctor to write you a prescription for problems such as this in the first chapter of Luke. The good doctor pens these words and they still provide healing for us today: "For with God nothing is impossible." When you decide to cherish family over everything else this world has to offer, you are on your way to true inner peace, a fruit of the Spirit more valuable than the largest diamond ever mined on this earth.

Let's explore a few questions that may help us in this vital area of life:

1. Do you allow your job or career to occupy an area of importance in your life greater than your family?

2. As relates to cherishing family, do you feel more guilt than peace?

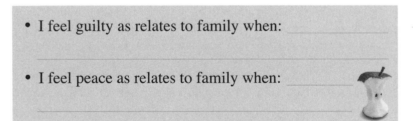

- I feel guilty as relates to family when: _____

- I feel peace as relates to family when: _____

3. On a scale of one to 10 with 10 being the very best, how would you rate yourself in the area of truly putting your family ahead of everything other than your relationship with God? Circle one: 1 2 3 4 5 6 7 8 9 10 What can you do to increase your number?

4. Do you have unresolved family issues in your past that keep you from putting your family first? If so, are you willing to get professional help in order to win a victory in this area of your life? Journal a paragraph about an unresolved family matter.

5. Would you be content to have God love and cherish you in the same proportion that you are currently loving and cherishing your family?

• My love for God is like: _____

• God's love for me is like: _____

Core Verses

📖 Put family above everything else. (Deuteronomy 4:25)

📖 Family is a gift from God. (Psalm 127)

📖 Family is a learning lab for life. (Proverbs 4:10)

📖 Functions of the family. (Colossians 3:18-20)

Action Steps for Implementing the Core Value
―――― "CHERISH FAMILY" ――――

🍎 We know that nobody gets to the end of their lives and says their only regret is that they didn't spend enough time at the office. Of course not, but many come to the end of their lives wishing they had spent more time cherishing their families. Make a decision today to put your family ahead of everything other than your relationship with Jesus.

Starting today, my family comes first.
Date _____ *Signed x*_____

🍎 Make a list of the ways you can start to cherish your family more over the next week, month, year and decade. Remember, some changes can happen right away but others may take time.

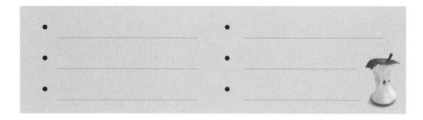

🍎 Ask God to help you mend broken family relationships where possible. Why not stop and pray now?

🍎 Decide now to set these three priorities in your life:
God first   Family second   Career third
Seek God's help to make it a reality.

🍎 Be quick to praise and slow to criticize members of your family. Vow to erase negative humor from your life especially as it relates to your family members.

PRAYER:

"Lord Jesus, be patient with me and teach me to love and cherish my family as much as you love and cherish me." Amen.

JOURNAL FOR THE WEEK:

"A happy family is but an earlier heaven." – Bowring

Chapter Four

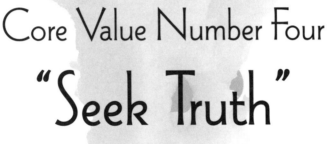

Core Value Number Four
"Seek Truth"

*"And you shall know the truth and
truth shall make you free."*
John 8:32

———————— "SEEK TRUTH" ————————

Zig Ziglar tells the story of a little first grade boy who responds with delight when his teacher asks the class to tell what they did over the weekend. The boy unwinds a tale of how he and his father went fishing over the weekend and caught 75 catfish, each weighing more than 75 pounds. The teacher corrects the boy, admonishing him to tell the truth. Over and over the boy insists the story is true. The teacher decides to tell a far-fetched story of her own as a means of teaching the boy a lesson. She says, "Johnny, what if I told you that on my way to school this morning a great big man-eating bear jumped out in front of my car and tore the door off, and just as he was about to eat me for breakfast, a little two-pound dog came out of the woods and jumped onto the bear and grabbed him by the nose and slammed the bear to the ground and killed him. Now Johnny, wouldn't you know that story was a lie?" To which Johnny quickly replied, "Oh no, Miss Honeycutt, I'd believe every word of it because that's my dog you're talking about."

Moral relativism (the concept that basically says whatever you think is true, is true) has been deeply woven into the fabric of our society. Many people have lost the entire concept of absolute truth. At the highest levels of our government, we were told that truth was only what you thought it to be. Remember the phrase from a former president of the United States, "that depends on what your definition of is, is." In order to seek truth, we need to understand the true meaning of truth. Jesus taught us the real meaning of truth with His words in the New Testament in the Gospel of John 16 when He said: "I am the way, the truth, and the life, no man comes to the Father except through Me." When Jesus used only three words to describe himself, one of the words was "truth" and it did not need to be parsed or come under the spell of a spin doctor. To understand truth, we must do our best to understand Jesus, the living God of truth. Jesus is the only person who ever walked on the earth who never told a lie. C. S. Lewis once said that Jesus either told the truth about who He was (the Son of God) or else He was either a lunatic or a liar. Our best way to learn anything is by imitation. We will be safe learning truth by simply imitating the life and work of Jesus. One of the greatest legacies we can have at the end of our lives is to be remembered for our honesty and integrity. If you have spent your life being an honest person, congratulations! If not, take heart; you can start today on the road to recovery and toward a lifetime of living like, and for, Jesus.

Let's explore a few thoughts about "seeking truth":

1. Would you consider yourself a regular or occasional liar? You laugh, but truth is truth. Would you consider yourself a moral relativist (someone who finds truth where it best fits their current situation)?

   ☐ I regularly lie (as needed)
   ☐ I occasionally lie (as needed)
   ☐ Everything is relative to the situation I find myself involved in.
   ☐ Lying comes naturally to me.
   ☐ I am always 100% honest no matter what!

2. Do you ever rationalize your view of truth by telling "little white lies" to either get what you want or avoid the difficulty of telling the truth?
   List a few reasons you do this.

   - _____
   - _____
   - _____
   - _____

3. How would you feel if you caught Jesus telling you a lie? Obviously you would be devastated. Can God really tell a lie? Study Titus 1:2 for the answer. How does this verse relate?

   _____
   _____
   _____
   _____

4. Do you hold others to a higher standard of truth than you hold for yourself?

- I expect my wife and kids to be ____% honest with me at all times.
- I expect my friends and coworkers to be ____% honest with me at all times.
- I expect my pastor or chaplain to be ____% honest with me at all times.

5. How many Bible verses can you list that have to do with truth and honesty? Which lies can you recall in the lives of the following Bible characters?

- Adam _____
- Noah _____
- David _____
- Ananias and his wife _____

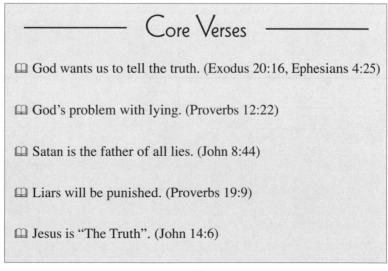

─────────── Core Verses ───────────

📖 God wants us to tell the truth. (Exodus 20:16, Ephesians 4:25)

📖 God's problem with lying. (Proverbs 12:22)

📖 Satan is the father of all lies. (John 8:44)

📖 Liars will be punished. (Proverbs 19:9)

📖 Jesus is "The Truth". (John 14:6)

Action Steps for Implementing the Core Value
———— "SEEK TRUTH" ————

Declare today as a lie-free day and do your best to go through the entire day without telling even a "little white one." Then try to chain together many days of truth in your life.

Ask God to help you understand what Jesus meant when He called himself "the truth." Search the true Word of God for its riches and truths.

Begin to see yourself as an honest person and affirm this fact in your self-talk.

- I can tell the truth.
- I am an honest person.
- I can tell the truth in love.

Catch your family being truthful and honest with you and congratulate them for it.

Establish an accountability relationship with someone based on mutual honesty. List potential accountability partners.

PRAYER:

"Lord Jesus, mentor me today in the depth of your truth."
Amen.

JOURNAL FOR THE WEEK:

"Truth and love are two of the most powerful things in the world; and when they both go together, they cannot easily be withstood." – Cudworth

Chapter Five

Core Value Number Five
"Share Christ"

"Ye are my witnesses, saith the LORD, and my servant
whom I have chosen: that ye may know and believe
me, and understand that I am he: before me there was
no God formed, neither shall there be after me. I, even
I, am the LORD; and beside me there is no saviour."
Isaiah 43:10-11

——————— "SHARE CHRIST" ———————

*O*ur world today is populated by close to 6.3 billion people. When we look at it as a real number, that's 6,300,000,000 and growing. If you had to guess, how many of that number do you think are evangelical Christians? Well, first of all, 1,200,000,000 are Muslims and another 1,500,000,000 are either Buddhist or Hindu. This means that close to half are parts of three non-Christian groups. More than a billion people on Earth profess no faith basis whatsoever. So, back to the question: Of the 6.3 billion people on the planet, how many are evangelical Christians? Would it shock you to know that a Christian think tank that very carefully tracks such matters records the number of true Christians on Earth to be as few as 252,000,000? Yes, Christians on planet Earth are a real genuine minority group. All that having been said, many people believe a true spiritual awakening is underway around the world today. This would not be inconsistent with what the Bible says will happen. In Acts 2, a prophecy from the Old Testament prophet Joel says God will indeed pour out His Spirit on the planet in the final days. If we take the Bible seriously, this could mean hundreds of millions could come to know Christ in our lifetime. So what should you do about it? That's simple; just share the Good News of Jesus as often as possible with as many people as possible. You say, "OK, but how, for crying out loud?"

A businessman in New York City in 1858 took this thought to heart and God used him to usher in a great spiritual awakening in the 19th century. His name was Jeremiah Lanphier, and he simply decided to start praying at lunchtime at his Wall Street office for God to bring about revival. He invited others to join him, and before long more than 30,000 people a day were praying for God's Spirit to be poured out. Guess what – it happened, and hundreds of thousands of people came to know Jesus in a personal way.

Coming out of the closet is not just an issue for fringe groups in our society. As Christians, we need to come out of the closet and tell people what our God means to us and what it is like to have a personal relationship with Jesus. Jesus said it best in another of His brilliantly brief statements. Basically, He said if we are ashamed to tell people about Him, He will be ashamed to tell His Father in Heaven about us. Can you imagine Jesus being ashamed of you? Of course not, so let's make a plan to add this very basic core value of "Sharing Christ" to our lives today.

Let's start by asking ourselves a few questions:

1. Would you characterize yourself as being "in" or "out" of the closet as relates to telling people about Jesus? Describe your reasoning for this answer.

2. Can you name anyone who will ultimately be in Heaven because you told them about Jesus this week, month, year, decade? List people who will be in heaven because you shared the "Good News" with them.

3. Do you think someone must be "gifted" in order to share Christ? If so, what made you come to this conclusion? Check the reasons you have for sharing Christ.

□ I can talk.
□ I breathe air.
□ I know Jesus.
□ I can tell what Jesus means to me.
□ I think Jesus can help my friends.
□ Jesus really wants me to tell people how to know Him.

4. What would your life be like today if there had never been a day that someone told you about Jesus?

☐ I really do not have an intimate relationship with Jesus.
☐ My life would be radically different without Jesus.
☐ I am not certain how to answer this question.

5. Are you ashamed of Jesus? Does He have reason to be ashamed of you? List the reasons or excuses you use to keep from "Sharing Christ".

- _____
- _____
- _____
- _____

Core Verses

📖 Eternal reason to share Christ. (2 Corinthians 5:10)

📖 Jesus is alive and is coming back to earth, we just do not know when. (Mark 13:32-37)

📖 You can have everything on earth, yet lose your soul. (Matthew 16:26-27)

📖 Sharing Jesus can bring much needed peace to your friends. (Matthew 11:28-30)

Action Steps for Implementing the Core Value
———— "SHARE CHRIST" ————

☰ Determine today that you will not go to Heaven alone. Make up your mind that with God's help, you will "come out of the closet" and start to make "Sharing Christ" a natural part of your life.

☰ Write down how you came to be in a personal relationship with Jesus and read it to yourself in the mirror until it sounds like something you can tell to a friend or stranger. If you have never come into a relationship with Jesus, turn to the next chapter of this book for the "Good News".

☰ Find someone who is having a genuine crisis in their life and tell them how Jesus can make a difference in their current drama. Then invite them to come into a personal relationship with Him like you did. Remember that 80% of all adults who come to faith in Christ do so during a moment of crisis.

☰ Find a solid Christian tract like Billy Graham's "Steps to Peace with God" or Campus Crusade for Christ's "Four Spiritual Laws" and become comfortable giving them to people and personally sharing the information they contain.

☰ Take a class that will teach you techniques for "Sharing Christ" and then integrate the things you learn into your daily life.

PRAYER:

"Lord Jesus, make me a true soul winner with power from on high and allow me to bring people to Heaven with me." Amen.

JOURNAL FOR THE WEEK:

"He who shall introduce into public affairs the principles of primitive Christianity, will revolutionize the world." – Franklin

Chapter Six

Celebrating Your
"Spiritual Birthday"

"For God so loved the world, that he gave his only begotten Son, that whosoever believeth in him should not perish, but have everlasting life."
John 3:16

*T*he God of the universe is interested not only in the events of this world but also the events of your life. God was aware of the day of your birth and it is His desire to see a second day of birth in your life, a spiritual birth.

We really can "Trust God". John 3:16 says, *"For God so loved the world that he gave his one and only Son, that whoever believes in him shall not perish but have eternal life."* (NIV)

The Bible teaches that we all need to experience and celebrate two birthdays. If you are reading this sentence, you are breathing air and if you are breathing air, you have experienced the first birth – the physical birth that occurred when you passed from your mother's womb and made your entrance into this world. The second birthday is a spiritual birth and one Jesus spoke of during a conversation with a leader named Nicodemus.

It is interesting to notice the number of leaders Jesus seemed to attract during his short time of ministry. Perhaps it was because He ran a thriving carpentry business himself. Perhaps his messages struck a chord with those who had achieved earthly success but found it wanting. Nevertheless, the New Testament provides a record of many successful people who were magnetically drawn to the life-changing Good News Jesus offered.

Nicodemus, a leader certainly looked up to by many, came to Jesus with far more questions than answers. He surrendered his pride and his position for a singular pursuit – a personal encounter with Jesus Christ. Perhaps you are reading this book with the same attitude Nicodemus had when he approached Jesus. Nicodemus recognized Jesus as a great leader and came to Jesus with words of praise for his wonderful works. He said, *"Rabbi, we know you are a teacher who has come from God. For no one could perform the miraculous signs you are doing if God were not with him."* (John 3:2 NIV) Perhaps, like Nicodemus, you know instinctively there is just something different about this man named Jesus that you have heard so much about. Perhaps, like Nicodemus, you know there has to be something more about Him than just a few good teachings, a few good works, and a few good morals. Perhaps you have had a family member tell you there is something more to be discovered about this man called Jesus.

While Nicodemus' words were true, they missed the real mark. Jesus' response to Nicodemus was a pointed change of subject. The New Testament records, *"In reply Jesus declared, 'I tell you the truth, no one can see the kingdom of God unless he is born again.'"* (John 3:3 NIV) Jesus brings the real mark into clear focus with a very direct and challenging statement sure to capture the attention of a mover and shaker like Nicodemus. No one goes to heaven unless he is born again. No one gets in "good with God" *unless he is born again.* No one fixes what is broken about life *unless he is born again.* But what do these words "born again" really mean?

Your personal reaction to the words of Jesus could vary. You could respond negatively based on stereotypes of people described as "born again believers." Your search for meaning to these words could be like that of Nicodemus, who responded with confusion and even more questions. While either response would be natural, the words of Jesus contain supernatural meaning. The Bible records this supernatural truth to a very natural response -- John 3:3-6: *"In reply Jesus declared, 'I tell you the truth, no one can see the kingdom of God unless he is born again.' 4 'How can a man be born when he is old?' Nicodemus asked. 'Surely he cannot enter a second time into his mother's womb to be born!' 5 Jesus answered, 'I tell you the truth, no one can enter the kingdom of God unless he is born of water and the Spirit. 6 Flesh gives birth to flesh, but the Spirit gives birth to spirit.'"* (NIV)

In other words, no one gets into heaven without experiencing two birthdays – a physical birthday first and a spiritual birthday second. Right now as you read the words on this page, a supernatural work may be occurring in your life. It is the same work that occurred in the life of Nicodemus more than 2,000 years ago. The Spirit may be giving birth to your spirit. While this work is supernatural, it is not complicated. Because the work is supernatural, you and I bring nothing but ourselves to the birthday party.

Maybe you are beginning to recognize what is true of every human being; we are all spiritually dead because of sin. Maybe you are starting to see sin for what it really is – an attempt to run life on our own terms independent of God. In essence, sin is you and I saying to God, "You run the world, and I'll run my own life." You may be recognizing the penalty for sin and, at the same time, realizing the solution. The penalty and the solution are summarized beautifully in one verse found in the New Testament book of Romans.

Romans 6:23 states, *"For the wages of sin is death, but the gift of God is eternal life in Christ Jesus our Lord."* (NIV) Like any gift, God's gift of life in and through Jesus is a gift to be received. It was a gift that caused Nicodemus, and hundreds of millions of others throughout history, to move beyond recognition to arms spread wide to receive the gift so freely offered by God. Jesus Christ is the gift you receive on your spiritual birthday.

Perhaps this book was a gift from a friend. Perhaps for the first time you are recognizing that you need a brand new birthday – a spiritual birthday. Perhaps today is the day for you to move from recognition to reception. Listen to the New Testament words of 2 Corinthians 6:2: *"For God says, 'At just the right time, I heard you. On the day of salvation, I helped you.' Indeed, God is ready to* help you right now. Today is the day of salvation." (NLT)

Wherever you are reading this, I invite you to bow your head and voice a simple prayer to God that will change your life forever.

"Jesus, I want a spiritual birthday. I know that I am helpless apart from You. I believe that only You can save me of my sins. Please come into my life for I believe that You died on my behalf at the cross, You went to the grave and You rose again. Father, I come to You alone with my sins, asking for forgiveness because I know I have disobeyed You throughout my entire life and only You have the power to change me. I praise You for sending Your only Son to save me. From now on, my life belongs to You so that whether I die right now, tomorrow, or years from now, I know I will be with You in heaven for eternity. Let me live for You all the days of my life, I pray in Christ's name. Amen."

If you sincerely prayed this prayer, let me be the first to say to you, "Happy Birthday!" Let me encourage you to write today's date on the spiritual birth certificate on page 44. While I am passing out encouragement, let me make one final suggestion. Share the news of your spiritual birthday with someone else, perhaps the person who gave you this book.

Guess what else is going on right now if you just prayed that prayer. The Bible states in Luke 15:10: *"In the same way, I tell you, there is joy in the presence of the angels of God over one sinner who repents."* (NASB) In other words, the angels in heaven are at this very moment holding a spiritual birthday party just for you!

Here is one more thing for you to think about following your decision to have a spiritual birthday. Just like your name was written down on your birth certificate at the hospital on the day of your physical (or water) birth, God has now written down your name on a spiritual birth certificate in what the Bible calls the *"Book of Life of the Lamb"* (Revelation 13:8 NKJV). And here is some really great news: your name is written in His book in the inerasable blood of Jesus. Take time right now to start your conversation with God by talking to him in prayer and thanking him for what He has just done in your life.

Now He wants you to go out and tell someone else what has just happened in your life. Jesus spoke directly to this point in the New Testament Gospel of Mark 8:38 when He said: *"For whoever is ashamed of Me and My words in this adulterous and sinful generation, of him the Son of Man also will be ashamed when He comes in the glory of His Father with the holy angels."* (NKJV) What person in their right mind would ever want Jesus to be ashamed of them? Of course, no one would, so do not be afraid to tell others that you have turned from your sin and trusted Jesus alone to be your God. Who knows? He may use your words to usher hundreds of millions into a real and vibrant relationship with Him.

41

Let's think about this eternally important matter:

1. When is your "Water Birthday"? _____ ___, _____
   Month Day Year

   Describe your favorite birthday party as a child.

2. What crisis is currently happening in your life that requires a God-sized solution?

   -
   -
   -
   -

3. Have you ever really had a "Spiritual Birthday" like the one written about in the preceding story? If so, try to write a single paragraph telling how it came about.

4. If not, can you make a list of things that are holding you back? List reasons you give for avoiding a relationship with Jesus.

- _____

- _____

- _____

- _____

5. Check the boxes below that represent the spiritual birthday present you would like to receive from Jesus.

☐ Joy   ☐ Love
☐ Peace   ☐ Eternal life
☐ Forgiveness   ☐ Rest
☐ Happiness   ☐ A good night's sleep
☐ Christian relationships

Core Verses

📖 Real peace comes from Jesus. (Romans 5:1)

📖 God loves us. (John 3:16)

📖 Why Jesus came to earth. (John 10:10)

📖 We are all sinners. (Romans 3:23)

📖 There is a price for sinning. (Romans 6:23)

📖 Our way will not work. (Proverbs 14:12)

📖 Jesus is the answer. (1 Timothy 2:5)

📖 Jesus' answer for our sin. (Romans 5:8)

📖 What happens when you believe. (John 1:12)

📖 How to confess your sin. (Romans 10:9)

📖 God's free gift (birthday present) of salvation. (Ephesians 2:8-9)

Action Steps for Celebrating Your
—— "SPIRITUAL BIRTHDAY" ——

🕯 Make this the day that you give up on being your own god.

🕯 Get down on your knees and sincerely pray the prayer listed on the previous page. All you need to do is:
- Admit you are a sinner apart from God.
- Openly turn from your sin.
- Believe Jesus died for your sins, rose from the grave and is alive today.
- Ask Jesus to take control of your life and fill you with His spirit.

🕯 Start today to fully trust God in every aspect of your life.

🕯 Go tell someone that you know is a Christian about your spiritual birthday and ask them to tell you about theirs.

🕯 Fill out the "Spiritual Birth Certificate" below. Drop to your knees once again and thank Jesus for what He has just done to transform your life.

Spiritual Birth Certificate

This Certificate hereby declares that, by placing my faith in Jesus Christ alone, I, _____ , celebrated my Spiritual
<small>New Believer's Name</small>

Birth on this ____ day of _____ , _____ .
<small>Day   Month   Year</small>

_____
<small>New Believer's Signature</small>

"In the same way, I tell you, there is rejoicing in the presence of the angels of God over one sinner who repents." **Luke 15:10 (NIV)**

"Lord Jesus, thank you for forgiving me of all my past sins. Show me the way to live for you for all of the days that I have left here on Earth. Please place people in my life who will help me grow from my spiritual birth into the mature believer who will be useful in your service." Amen.

JOURNAL FOR THE WEEK:

"To be born once is the definition of life, to be born again is the reality of eternal life" – Anonymous

— Chapter Seven —

Core Value Number Six
"Expect Miracles"

"If you have faith as a grain of mustard seed, you will say to this mountain, 'Move from here to there,' and it will move and nothing will be impossible for you."
Matthew 17:20

"EXPECT MIRACLES"

As much as you expect to take a breath the first thing tomorrow morning when you wake up, you should expect miracles to occur in your life during the balance of the day. The simple process of taking that first breath in the morning is in itself a miracle. Too many times in life we expect miracles to be these far out supernatural events from a "Ripley's Believe It Or Not" program. Just the opposite is true. Miracles are truly happening in our lives every day, and often we take them for granted. The fact that most of us can walk, talk, smell, touch, and see is miraculous. However, even greater miracles are also occurring all around us, and all we need to do is expect them from a God who is in the business of creating them. Everything about Jesus is miraculous, from His virgin birth to His resurrection from the tomb and everything in the middle, from everything that happened before and since all those events. The fact that He created us in His own image and likeness is astounding and miraculous. His promise in Psalm 91 that angels will protect us to the point that our foot will not even slip is a miracle. The way He has elected to speak to us through the Bible is a miracle. His promise of transforming us following our true heartfelt belief in Him as the Savior of the world is a miracle. In addition to that, His promise to place His Holy Spirit into our lives to help us while we struggle here on Earth is a miracle. The ability all of us have to talk to God through prayer (even if we all chose to do it at the same time) is a miracle. The ability He has given us to reason with our minds through the great and small issues of life is a miracle.

How about this universe He created for us to live in? It miraculously contains all the elements we need not only to survive but also to thrive and prosper and sense His presence to the fullest. The fact that He creates every one of us as totally unique all the way down to our DNA and fingerprints is indeed a miracle. However, one of the most miraculous things of all is the fact that some day we will leave this earth and have the opportunity to spend the balance of all eternity with Him in a place called Heaven, where we will see miracles beyond our ability to even think about. Heaven is a place where we will see streets actually made of pure gold and seas as clear as crystal.

God wants us to ask for, and expect, miracles in our ordinary lives every day. The Bible tells us that nothing is impossible with God, and that with just the smallest amount of faith, we can see the greatest of all miracles. Expecting miracles in our lives should be as simple as waking up in the morning and taking that first wonderful breath of the day.

Questions we should discuss about the miraculous:

1. Do miracles have to be big, huge, unexplainable, supernatural events in order to get your attention? List as many of Jesus' miracles as you can remember.

- _____
- _____
- _____
- _____

2. What miracles have you experienced in the last five years, five months, five weeks, five days, five hours, or five minutes?

- _____
- _____
- _____
- _____

3. Can big-time miracles like the parting of the Red Sea still happen today? Why or why not? Read Luke 1:37 and fill in these blanks. Then answer the question above in light of the context of the verse.
   F _ _ W _ _ _ G _ _ N _ _ _ _ _ _ I _ I _ _ _ _ _ _ _ _ _.
   Now memorize this verse and say it at least 10 times a day!

4. How do the following miracles found in the Bible relate to you?

* Creation story in Genesis _____
* Noah and the flood _____
* Daniel and the lion's den _____
* The virgin birth of Jesus _____
* The resurrection of Christ from the dead _____
* Jesus raising Lazarus from the dead _____
* Paul raising the dead boy _____
* Jesus forgiving the woman caught in adultery _____

5. What kind of miracles do you need in your life today? Choose the categories that you need a miracle in and list the exact needs.

☐ Health _____

☐ Relationships _____

☐ Finances _____

☐ Spiritual _____

☐ Career _____

——— Core Verses ———

📖 God can do anything. (Luke 1:37)

📖 Angels can do miracles for us. (Psalm 91:11-12)

📖 Jesus' first recorded miracle. (John 2)

📖 David kills the giant. (1 Samuel 17:1-58)

📖 Jesus controls the weather. (Matthew 8:23-27)

📖 Jesus heals people. (John 5:1-15)

📖 Big miracle after Jesus goes back to heaven. (Acts 16:16-40)

Action Steps for Implementing the Core Value
—— "EXPECT MIRACLES" ——

🍎 Start a miracle notebook and simply list the amazing things, big or little, God does in your life every day.

🍎 Take some time in the next week to simply reflect on the miracles that have occurred in your life to this point.

🍎 Start each day, as soon as you wake, thanking God for the miracle of life.

🍎 Ask God to help you expect miracles to happen and reveal them to you as they happen.

🍎 Begin a study of the New Testament and list every miracle you encounter. You may wish to do this over a long period of time in conjunction with other Bible studies. You may wish to have a friend join in this effort with you.

PRAYER:

"Lord Jesus, please help me to recognize a miracle when I see one and to expect one all the time." Amen.

JOURNAL FOR THE WEEK:

"Every believer is God's miracle." – Bailey

— Chapter Eight —

Core Value Number Seven
"Be Grateful"

*"In everything, give thanks, for this is the will
of God in Christ Jesus for You."*
I Thessalonians 5:18

"BE GRATEFUL"

*T*here were two words or phrases many of us learned as kids that were often called the "magic words" by our moms and dads: "please" and "thank you". Most of the time we had to recite these words to get the treat or as a result of receiving one. Failing to offer up the magic words might have carried greater consequences than missing out on a treat, however. It had the potential of resulting in a mystical tingling sensation to our backsides. Our parents, however, were really doing us a big favor by trying to teach us to be grateful. They were actually teaching us about God's faithfulness, His grace, and His mercy.

When we fail to be grateful, we rob ourselves of one of life's great blessings. But do not be deceived; true gratefulness comes from the heart, not the head. It is much more than reciting a phrase. The simple act of expressing gratitude says something about our inner character. Some of the most grateful people on earth also happen to be the ones who give the most. Why do they know what so many others seem to miss? Maybe they are living just a little closer to the kind of life Jesus lived here on Earth. Even though He owned everything in existence, Jesus went to extraordinary lengths to show His gratitude. He was so thankful when the little boy was willing to give away his lunch that He took the contents of the small lunch pail to feed thousands of hungry people. Even though He was God in the flesh here on Earth, He thanked His Father in Heaven during his public and private prayers. If an "attitude of gratitude" was good enough for Jesus, how much better must it be for us?

When employees who have quit their jobs are surveyed for reasons they felt compelled to make a change, many simply stated that they didn't feel appreciated for the work they were doing. This may seem like a little thing until you consider that the cost of rehiring and retraining the average worker costs more than $10,000. Or even worse, many times when interviewed following a divorce, people say they gave up on their marriages because their spouses never showed them any appreciation.

When we develop an attitude of gratefulness, we truly draw closer to God. How odd it seems to lift new intercessory prayers to God when we have not been grateful for His provisions of the past.

Things to think about regarding gratitude:

1. Do you consider yourself to be a truly grateful person? List ways, large or small, that you have shown gratitude this week.

2. Who are some people you know who demonstrate "attitudes of gratitude" and how do they do it?

3. When was the last time you truly thanked someone for something they did for you? Explain the circumstances of the event.

4. When was the last time that gratitude was demonstrated toward you? Explain the circumstances.

5. Do you view gratitude as a learned skill or a talent? What causes you to think this?

Core Verses

📖 Pray with a grateful heart. (Philippians 4:6)

📖 Be thankful for what God gives you. (1 Timothy 4:3-5)

📖 Gratitude is even shown in heaven. (Revelation 4:9)

📖 Be thankful for everything. (Ephesians 5:20)

📖 Why we give thanks before a meal. (Romans 14:6)

Action Steps for Implementing the Core Value
——— "BE GRATEFUL" ———

🍎 Make a list of all the things you have to be grateful for.

🍎 Sometime in the next hour, find a way to show gratitude to someone.

🍎 Have a goal to become known as a grateful person.

🍎 Make sure your prayers every day include thanksgiving for His provision and ask Him to create in you an "attitude of gratitude."

🍎 Develop phrases that become part of your life that exemplify thanksgiving and use them every day.

PRAYER:

"Lord Jesus, first I thank you for all the amazing things you have done for me. Now I ask you to create in me an 'attitude of gratitude'." Amen.

JOURNAL FOR THE WEEK:

"He who receives a benefit should never forget it; he who bestows should never remember it." – Charron

Chapter Nine

Core Value Number Eight
"Simplify Everything"

"But I fear that somehow you will be led away from
your pure and simple devotion to Christ, just as
Eve was deceived by the serpent."
II Corinthians 11:3 (NLT)

—— "SIMPLIFY EVERYTHING" ——

*H*ave you ever thought about how to define pure genius? A true
genius is someone who can take the most complicated subject on Earth
and reduce it to the ridiculously sublime in a matter of seconds. The
Bible teaches us a lot about this subject, and much of this is visible in the
life of Jesus. In John 4:11, Jesus learned that his longtime friend Lazarus
died. Other friends compelled Jesus to come to the funeral to care for the
grievers. He decided to walk to the city where Lazarus died, which took
a few days. By the time He arrived, He found his friend had already been
buried. Instead of going through the complicated process of helping all
the friends and family work through the five stages of grief, He simply
raised Lazarus from the dead. You may say, "That's easy for Jesus, but
I can't just go around raising people from the dead." Well, of course
not because you aren't God in flesh like Jesus. But there are plenty of
complicated things that pop in your life every day that can be handled
much more efficiently by a process of simplification. Here is some good
news on this subject. Becoming a genius in this area of life is a learned
skill and not a God-given talent. You can learn how to simplify things in
your life, and in so doing, your own quality of life will soar as a result.

The phrase "less is more" is often used in business, and it adequately
illustrates the point of simplifying things in our lives. What it is really
saying is quite profound. The more things we have, the more we become a slave to things. Yet the fewer things we have, the more time and
energy we have to truly live life. Isn't it interesting that Jesus didn't tie
Himself down with things? What makes this even more fascinating is
the fact that He created all things and truly owned all things, yet they
had no hold on Him. What an example for us today! As far as we can
tell, Jesus did it all without committee meetings, bankers, spreadsheets,
computers, PDA's, cable or satellite television, a car or truck, a boat or
house of His own, a wrist watch, an Armani suit, a jet plane, pens and
pencils, a leather brief case, a monogrammed shirt, a diamond ring, sil-
ver and china, an electric razor, Gatorade, the NFL, NBA, NHL, NCAA,
or even the WWE. How could He ever play God without all this stuff?
That's easy; He doesn't have to play God – He is God. If He can get by
just fine by simplifying life, so can we. The more we emulate Jesus, the
more peace we will have in our lives. How much would you be willing to give up to truly enjoy the peace that passes all understanding?

Here are some simple questions to ponder:

1. What "things" in your life require more effort than they are worth? Make a list.

- _____
- _____
- _____
- _____

2. How do you feel about your ability to apply simple solutions to complicated problems?

☐ I do it all the time.
☐ I have never given it any thought.
☐ I need help in this area of my life.
☐ I tend to overcomplicate even the simplest of matters.

3. How might your life be different if you were to simplify certain aspects of it? Choose one of the following areas of life and write your thoughts: finances, relationships, work, lifestyle, family.
   If I were to simplify my_____ , then I would have more _____ .

4. How can you apply the "less is more" principle to your life? List your thoughts.

☐ Family _____

☐ Relationships _____

☐ Finances _____

☐ Lifestyle _____

☐ Career _____

5. How do you rank yourself in the area of mental and material clutter?

☐ In need of an "Extreme Makeover".
☐ Some need for improvement.
☐ I am hiding my need for help in this area.
☐ I do a good job in this area.
☐ I want to improve in this area of my life.

Core Verses

📖 Simplifying worries. (Matthew 6:34)

📖 Finding peace in the clutter. (Philippians 4:6-7)

📖 Stillness overcomes over activity. (Psalm 37:7)

📖 God will make sure you have just enough of what you need. (Matthew 6:25-26)

📖 God can do more for us than we can do for ourselves. (Ephesians 3:20)

Action Steps for Implementing the Core Value
— "SIMPLIFY EVERYTHING" —

🍎 Make a commitment to start today to simply your life.

🍎 Ask God to help you through the process by prompting you with simple solutions to complicated problems.

🍎 Spend time every day engaging in "less is more" self talk.

🍎 Encourage a friend to join you in the process of simplification.

🍎 Make a list of areas of your life that will benefit and thrive through simplification. Then place it on the refrigerator and read it every morning.

I am asking God to simplify the following areas of my life:

- _____
- _____
- _____
- _____
- _____
- _____
- _____
- _____
- _____
- _____
- _____
- _____

PRAYER:

"Lord Jesus, please allow me to be more like you and less like me every day." Amen.

JOURNAL FOR THE WEEK:

"The measure of a person is not how much it takes to make them happy, but how little." – Anonymous

— Chapter Ten —

Core Value Number Nine
"Regret Nothing"

*"Do not remember the former things, nor
consider the things of old."*
Isaiah 43:18

———— "REGRET NOTHING" ————

A life full of regrets can be paralyzing. Particularly when you consider they serve no useful purpose whatsoever. Every minute of our lives we spend in the "coulda, shoulda, woulda" mode is a precious minute of life lost forever. Even worse, it's a minute invested in failure. Investments are designed to pay dividends; the dividends reaped from negative investments always result in greater loss to the investor. In other words, regrets cause us to dig a deep hole even deeper, often to the point of making it almost impossible to climb out of the hole.

So, big deal, you have done some things in life you wish you hadn't. Do you think that makes you more special than the rest of us? Get real! Every person who has ever lived has things in their lives they would certainly do differently the second time around. The greatest benefits from the mistakes of our past are the valuable lessons we derive from them. You can never see the brilliant future God has in store for you if you are always focused on your rear view mirror. Besides, if you are constantly looking to the rear, you are likely to crash into something new coming from the front.

Let's focus for a moment on Adam, the first person talked about in the Bible. Now here are two examples of how regretting the past would present a big problem. Adam himself could have spent the rest of his life regretting the apple incident. Moreover, God could have Himself fallen into regret for ever creating Adam in the first place. However, the Bible contains no evidence of either being the case. We have no record of Adam or God wasting time regretting the apple incident. Both simply shouldered the consequences of the action and moved on with the development of the world. God teaches us a great lesson here about leaving our regrets behind. What if God had wasted a lot of time regretting He ever created Adam? Guess what, if He had, you probably wouldn't be reading this right now. Everybody makes mistakes. Isn't it interesting that God could have wasted time regretting the future because He knew about the apple incident before He ever created Adam in the first place? Yet it didn't stop Him from loving us enough to keep focusing forward to the day His Son would come to redeem all our regrets on the Cross. That's right, no matter what your regrets might be, Jesus died for them once and for all. So why not trust Him to forgive the past and help you stay focused on the future?

Let's think more about regrets:

1. What are the things in your life you need to wipe clean from your memory in order to be able to move forward with God?

- _____
- _____
- _____
- _____

2. These people in the Bible struggled with regrets. Can you name some of their problems?

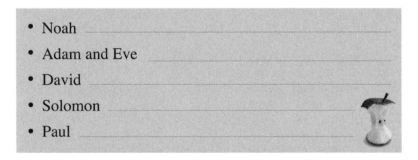

- Noah _____
- Adam and Eve _____
- David _____
- Solomon _____
- Paul _____

3. Are there examples in the lives of these same Biblical figures that show how they put their past in perspective and went on to accomplish great things for the Kingdom of God?

- _____
- _____
- _____
- _____

4. Do the scales of your life tip heavier in the area of regret or hope for the future? Why is one side weightier than the other? Explain why you feel this way.

5. Do you think it is humanly possible to let go of your regrets? If not, do you have enough faith to allow God to take them from you? If God can forget your mistakes, why are you unable to? In what areas will you need God's help?

Core Verses

📖 Jesus will turn our sorrows into joy. (John 16:20)

📖 Jesus warned against regretting what would happen on the cross. (Luke 23:28)

📖 Regrets will lead to physical ailments. (Psalm 31:9-10)

📖 God will replace our past sorrows with love and joy. (Psalm 32:10-11)

Action Steps for Implementing the Core Value
—— "REGRET NOTHING" ——

☕ Make a list of the many things in life you spend time regretting.

- _____
- _____
- _____
- _____

- _____
- _____
- _____
- _____

☕ Take a small metal ash can outside and burn the list. (Since this may be a bit dangerous, why not cross through each one right now and ask God to keep these regrets from hindering you again.)

☕ Resolve not to invest another minute in the "coulda, shoulda, woulda" mode. Instead, focus on future goals.

☕ Begin today to develop a future oriented attitude about life. If a regret from the past pops into your head, immediately ask Jesus to take it from you.

☕ Write the following statement on an index card and tape it to your bathroom mirror and read it every time you look in the mirror.

"Jesus died for my past regrets, and I have no right to hang Him on the cross for them again. Therefore I will accept His free grace and move forward with great hope in the future."

"Lord Jesus, thank you for knowing my regrets before I was born, dying for them on the cross, and freeing my mind to move forward without their pain." Amen.

JOURNAL FOR THE WEEK:

"Has this world been so kind to you that you should leave with regret? There are better things ahead than any we leave behind." – C. S. Lewis

— Chapter Eleven —

Core Value Number Ten
"Pray Now"

"Pray without ceasing."
I Thessalonians 5:17

"PRAY NOW"

*T*here once lived a man named John Hyde who could teach us all a thing or two about praying. Though he's been dead for almost 100 years, a "Google" search on his name uncovers close to 1,400 hits. His fame even after death is a direct result of his basic communication and conversations with God. At one point in his 20 years of missionary work in India, he became known as the Apostle of Prayer. Later they called him "the man who never sleeps", but finally they simply called him "the praying Hyde". Obviously he took the words of the Holy Spirit, delivered by the Apostle Paul in I Thessalonians 5:17, very seriously. When he talked to God, things happened. People who observed him in prayer were often moved to tears by the reality of his open communion with the God of the universe. He died February 17, 1912, and his last words were, "Shout the victory of Jesus Christ!" What would it take to be just like "praying Hyde"? Would one have to qualify by education? No. Age? No. Race? No. Height or weight? No. Marital status? No. Wealth? No. Voice quality? No. Career status? No. If not by these things, then what? Very simply, it takes just two things: spiritual desire and time.

Some of the prayers we offer up today would probably make Hyde cry but not in the same way his prayers made people of his day cry. Where did we come up with the idea that we need to turn all sanctimonious and pray in old King James English in order for God to hear us? Here's a news flash: we don't have a record in the Bible of Jesus using a bunch of "thee's" and "thou's" when He talked to God in prayer. He simply talked to Him like I would talk to my earthly dad, and God wants us to talk to Him the same way and often. Not just before a meal or once a day before bedtime. God wants to talk to us all the time. He created us to have a relationship with him that is day by day, hour by hour, minute by minute and second by second. In our conversation with God, we are never alone.

The very minute we hear a prayer request, we should lift it before God. Waiting may have disastrous consequences. God is always ready to hear and answer our prayers. He even chides us in the Bible when He says, "I haven't answered you because you haven't asked me." If you were to call the president of the United States and ask the telephone operator to get the President on the line for you, there is little chance you will speak with him. But you can stop anytime and speak directly with the God of the universe with no appointment and talk about the simplest or most complicated matters. All He wants is a relationship with you. So the next time someone asks you to pray about something, stop whatever you are doing and "Pray Now."

Discussion thoughts about "Praying Now":

1. Would your friends and family consider you a person of prayer? Why or why not?

2. If you compared the amount of time you spend in prayer each day with the following modes of transportation, which best describes you? Circle one of the following, then write your explanation below.

   Skateboard   Mini-bike   SUV   Ferrari   Hummer

3. When you have a most urgent personal need in your life, whom do you call on to pray about the matter? Why this person or group of people?

Person or group: _____

Why them? _____

4. Describe the most moving prayer time of your entire life.

My most memorable prayer time was when: _____

_____

_____

The result was: _____

5. Do you have an active daily "Prayer List"? Write the items that should be on your daily prayer list below.

- _____   - _____   - _____

- _____   - _____   - _____

- _____   - _____   - _____

- _____   - _____   - _____

Core Verses

📖 The Lord's Prayer. (Matthew 6:9-13)

📖 Pray continually. (1 Thessalonians 5:17-18)

📖 Prayers answered. (Psalm 66:13-20)

📖 Evidence of God answering prayers on behalf of friends. (Acts 12:5)

📖 God hears our prayers. (Psalm 34:15-18)

📖 Pray and continue to work. (Nehemiah 4:9)

📖 Pray without doubt. (James 1:6)

Action Steps for Implementing the Core Value
——— "PRAY NOW" ———

🍎 Stop right now and make a real "Prayer List".

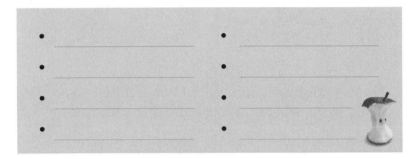

- ————————— - —————————
- ————————— - —————————
- ————————— - —————————
- ————————— - —————————

🍎 Start today to see prayer as being as essential as the oxygen you breathe. Take in a breath right now, and immediately stop and thank God for it.

🍎 The very next time someone asks you to pray about something, stop immediately and do it. Develop a "do it now" philosophy about prayer.

🍎 Ask God today to reveal Himself more deeply to you through your prayer life.

🍎 Find a copy of a book about John Hyde or George Muller. Read them as soon as possible and begin to emulate their lives.

- **John Hyde: Apostle of Prayer (Men of Faith)** *by Francis McGaw (less than $3 on Amazon.com)*
- **George Muller: Man of Faith & Miracles: A Biography of One of the Greatest Prayer-Warriors of the Past Century** *by Basil Miller (less than $2 on Amazon.com)*

PRAYER:

"Lord Jesus, create in my heart a passion for devotion to communion with you through prayer. Let me be the John Hyde of the 21st century so that people will refer to me as 'the praying _____'." Amen.

JOURNAL FOR THE WEEK:

"He who prays as he ought will endeavor to live as he prays." – Owen

— Chapter Twelve —

What is the Conclusion of the Matter?
"Conclusion"

"Here is the conclusion of the matter"
Ecclesiastes 12:13 (NIV)

"CONCLUSION"

What is the conclusion of the entire matter? For the answer to this question, we can look once again to one of the wisest people in the Bible, Solomon. He was a guy who had seen it all, done it all, had it all and practically knew it all. He might have been the only person in the Old Testament who could have actually beaten Ken Jennings at Jeopardy. As his life was drawing to a close, he began to reflect on his past as many people do in their twilight years. The Holy Spirit of God thought these reflections were significant enough to allow them to be recorded in the Bible in the book of Ecclesiastes. After 12 chapters of Solomon reflecting back over his life, we finally receive the following as his last recorded thoughts about life: "Now all has been heard; here is the conclusion of the matter: Fear God and keep his commandments, for this is the whole duty of man. For God will bring every deed into judgment including every hidden thing whether it is good or evil." (Ecclesiastes 12:13-14 NIV)

Unquestionably, it will be much easier for us to "fear God and keep His commandments" if we have established a livable, workable set of "core values" for our lives. The "core values" we have committed to in this study are not good just for the long term for reflection during our last days on Earth. They weave the fabric that truly places us squarely in a "day by day, hour by hour, minute by minute, second by second" relationship with the same God of the universe that Solomon worshipped. When we have fully integrated these "core values" into our lives, the net result will be the overpowering "Fruit of the Spirit" promised in Galatians 5. The Bible is true and real when it promises that whatever we sow in life, we will also reap. Now, at the conclusion of this study, we are well on our way to reaping a lifetime of "love, joy, peace, patience, kindness, goodness, faithfulness, gentleness, and self-control." Wow! How cool is that? When we take an in-depth look at the life of Solomon, we can clearly see that even though he was the smartest guy on the planet, he was missing some of these "core values." How differently might the book of Ecclesiastes been written if he had integrated all of them into his life at an early age? Regardless of what Solomon may or may not have done, we can make a proactive decision to do it now!

Action Steps for the Conclusion of the Matter
—— "CONCLUSION" ——

Ⓣ Drop to your knees right now and ask God to draw near to you in a "day by day, hour by hour, minute by minute, second by second" relationship with Him.

Ⓣ Come out of the closet, close the door behind you, and lock it forever.

Ⓣ Breathe in the freedom of a life fully committed to Jesus Christ.

Ⓣ Commit to tell anyone who will listen how Jesus can also change his or her life forever.

Ⓣ Memorize your "core values" and review them often.

Ⓣ Study your Bible daily for new ways to deepen your relationship with Jesus.

Ⓣ Talk to God constantly about the largest and smallest details of your life.

Ⓣ Take a group of five to 10 friends through this study over the next couple of months and then repeat the process as often in the year as you can.

Ⓣ Keep your focus on the future, remembering that our time on earth right now is simply a vapor or, as Solomon said in Ecclesiastes, "grasping at the wind."

Ⓣ Keep your eyes focused on Jesus, knowing that humans may let us down but Jesus never will.

PRAYER:

"Lord Jesus, please make these "core values" a permanent part of my life and use them to magnify the fruit of your Holy Spirit in my life in ways that will amaze me every day for the rest of my life." Amen.

LET US HEAR FROM YOU:

If God has indeed used this project to change you in some way, please let us know about it by visiting our website at **www.iamchap.org**. Click the picture of the "Twenty Words" book and leave us your thoughts in the space provided.

May God richly bless you for investing your time, energy, and efforts in the pages of this book. I pray He has instilled in you a set of "core values" that will change your life forever.

Twenty Words That Have Changed My Life Forever

1. Trust God
2. Love People
3. Cherish Family
4. Seek Truth
5. Share Christ
6. Expect Miracles
7. Be Grateful
8. Simplify Everything
9. Regret Nothing
10. Pray Now

If at all possible, print these 10 core values on the back of your business card. They serve as a constant reminder for yourself as well as a witnessing tool for others.